1

FLOUR SACK BLOOMERS

BY

Lucy Fetterhoff

© 2001 by Lucy Fetterhoff

Dedicated to my son, Ed.

Table of Contents

Sister Cecile's Wedding 13

The Lil Man in the Machine 33

Plucks, Cracks and Fatback 41

Watch the Birdie 65

Ballard's Best Goes to School 89

The Writing on the Kitchen Wall 99

Back From the Golden West 127

Lucy Fetterhoff was a skinny little schoolgirl back in the late 1920's when she wrote this book at her desk in the little one-room school she attended.

That penciled manuscript gathered dust in the attic through the Great Depression, World War II, and all those tumultuous years in the rest of the 20th Century.

That skinny kid is now in her 90's. She recently blew the dust off FLOUR SACK BLOOMERS and shares that life with us now in this brand new century.

Grey hairs have visited the head of that little girl as well as the heads of her children and grandchildren since these words were written.

The reader is invited to slip back a few decades to visit those times.

Sister Cecile's Wedding

One Sunday morning just after breakfast, Sister Cecile said she had a surprise for us -- she and Toady had made up their minds to wed. Naturally, this set off quite a to-do at our house. Sister Cecile's announcement made Ma cry, but she stopped her tears to say she'd sell enough eggs and butter to get Sister Cecile the dress of her dreams to be married in, "even if I have t' squeeze ever' last one of th' chickens an' cows myself!"

Aint Jidy told Sister Cecile, "Young lady, ye waited a mighty long time t' speak yore mind. Hit's a wonder t' me ye wuz able t' keep Toady danglin' on th' line as long as ye did" Sister Cecile just tossed her head from side to side and laughed at Aint Jidy's comment.

"How DID ye git Toady t' pop th' question?" Amy asked.

"Oh, hit wuz easy as enythin'," Sister Cecile answered, "once't I wuz set in my mind thet he wuz th' one fer me, I knew he warn't ever gonter marry up with any other."

"Have patience, Amy," Ma said, "Rufus'll come t' his senses, one o' these days."

When Toady came to court Sister Cecile that Sunday afternoon, he sought out Pa on the front porch and had a long talk with him. I couldn't make out what was said, but when they came inside Pa said Toady could come calling on Sister Cecile on Wednesday nights, too.

14

"I know jest how hit is with ye," Pa was saying as they came in from the porch to join us, "I wuz so anxious t' set with Phobe here before we wed, I thought th' day would never come 'till th' Preacher tied th' knot. I tell ye, Missus Pine, was as fine a young lady as ye'd ever hope to set yer eyes, "Pa went on, "I swear I must'a fooled her some way t' git her t' marry me," he said with a wink in Ma's direction.

"Cain't tell me which one of ye got fooled worse tha t'other 'un," Aint Jidy was quick to chime in, "seems like iffen ye put th' two o'

15

ye in a poke t'gether an' shook it real hard, hit'd be a guess which would would fall out first."

That set everyone to laughing and then to teasing Toady. He instantly turned bright red from the neck up and that made us laugh all the more. It wasn't long before he and Sister Cecile escaped for a walk down the path past the spring house.

The weeks which followed were busy ones for everyone. Ma seemed to be everywhere at once, cleaning, cooking, and preparing for Sister Cecile's big day. Pa told her, "Phoebe, ye'd better slow yerself down, ye been busier than a bumble bee in a bucket of tar!"

Ma set down the big cardboard box she was carrying and set it in her room behind the door. This, she said, was Sister Cecile's "wedding box." Into it would go all the things that were given to the bride for her wedding day.

The following day, Ma and Aint Jidy went to Echo City and bought some plisse crepe to make Sister Cecile some night gowns. We usually slept in our drawers and petticoats and we all understood you only got nightgowns when you got married.

"I had me a prutty nightgown when me an yor Pa wuz married," Ma told Sister Cecile as they sat sewing on the material. "But hit soon wore out an' I bin sleepin' in my chimmy ever since."

"Ma, did you miss not havin' a nightgown?" Amy asked.
"Yes," she sighed, " I wish't I'd been able t' have two enyhow. Maybe they wouldn't a wore out so soon."
"I'm gon'ter have mor'n two, Ma, " Sister Cecile declared from where she sat by the window. "I'm gon'ter have four, an' that's more'n almost anyone ever had, aint hit, Ma?"

"Yes, yes," Ma replied, "an' Sister Cecile I want ye t' take care o' thim so when ye have young'uns, ye'll have somethin' nice t'wear when you walk through th' Valley o' th' Shadow o' Death."

"Ma, why do ye allus call hit th' Valley o' th' Shadow o' Death?" Sister Cecile wanted to know.

"Well, I reckon," Ma told her, "ye have t' figger a woman has gone t' th' Gates of Heaven when she's havin' a baby. Pore ol' Myrt Homingjohn never made hit an' both her an' her young'un passed on."

"Sister Cecile, how many young' uns are you an' Toady gon'ter have?" Lily-May asked with a sly smile.

Aint Jidy gave her a resounding smack on her behind and told Lily-May to go outside, or find herself something worthwhile to do. Then she explained, "Sister Cecile will take what th' Good Lord sends her, an' she won't be particular whether they're boys 'er girls, nor how they look neither. But let's all wait til th' weddin' knot is tied good an' tight b'fore we hcar enymore talk 'bout startin' a family."

As she left the room, Lily-May said, "well, Aint Suzy said iffen ye eat an apple an' spit out th' seeds an' slap 'em on yer forehead, how ever many stick'll be th' number of children ye'll have."

"My word, there's no tellin' whut on earth thet young'un gon'ter say next!" Aint Jidy rolled her eyes and Sister Cecile smiled.

Over the following days the news of the wedding spread. Soon, folks started bringing a little gift to put in Sister Cecile's Wedding Box. Of course, everyone wanted to know all about Sister Cecile's and Toady's plans and all their friends in the holler and in Echo City said they planned to come to the wedding.

Anyone could see that Sister Cecile loved all the attention and fussing over her and she was always eager to offer details about the wedding arrangements. She told Louellen Perru, "Toady is goin' t' have a house raisin' an as soon as hit is built, we will be wed."

"Toady's Pa an' Ma done right well by him," Ma would add, "they gived him a piece o' nice land 'bout a whoop an' a holler b'low their place, an' Toady said he wuz goin' t' have a home fer Sister Cecile th' day she becomes his wife."

"Now, aint that real fine," Missus Biggers said when she came to get her butter, and her share of the news about the coming event. She decided to spend the afternoon helping Ma and Aint Jidy sew on Sister Cecile's quilt, the "Double Wedding Ring".

"Hit shure is a good name for a quilt fer someone who is gittin' married," Ma said.

"I got this ring when I got married to Mr. Biggers," Missus Biggers replied and held out her hand for admiring glances. It was a band ring and solid gold, she said.

Knowing Ma didn't have a ring, Sister Cecile said, "I don't want a ring. I told Toady to take th' $5.69 that they cost and buy things fer th' new house."

It wasn't long before the little two-room house was completed, but then Sister Cecile and Toady surprised everyone by announcing they had decided to postpone the wedding day until their house could be furnished.

Ma invited the neighbor women over for an entire day to help make curtains, sheets and pillow cases. Toady's Ma gave the couple a feather bed so then Ma chased down several of the geese in the chip yard and robbed them of their feathers. She got enough to make Sister Cecile a pair of pillows, and explained with satisfaction afterwards, "I jest don't want Missus Stumpgate t' think I cain't give th' bride an' groom somethin' nice, too."

"Phoebe," Pa scolded her, "yer jest showin' off 'cause Toady's Ma saw th' geese when she was hyar last Sunday 'fore last. I set right there in thet chur an' told her ye had nine geese."

"Where wuz I at, I didn't hear her?" Ma wanted to know.

"I think ye wuz in the spring-house bringing up th' milk fer dinner," Pa answered.

"Well, th' pillow is made an' when the Preacher marries thim Sunday they'll have a house o' their own t' go to and hit'll be furnished" Ma said with a satisfied look.

Sunday Morning all of us were up early without Ma calling us. Sister Cecile was the last to come to the table for her final breakfast as a "single lady" and according to the proper way of doing things, we all stood as she took her seat next to Ma.

"Happy is th' Bride that th' sun shineth on," Aint Jidy said, and I thought to myself, if it was raining, Aint Jidy would have told us a bride in a wet dress will have a happy marriage.

"It shure looks like hit gon'ter be a pretty day , fer th' light streaks are in th' West," Pa announced.

"How do ye feel?" Amy asked Sister Cecile

"Oh, I feel jest like any other day,' Sister Cecile answered her, 'ceptin' I'm nervous as a crow's foot."

"Now, child," Ma said, " hit's natural fer ye t' feel like thet, so don't ye think eny more 'bout hit."

"Ma, Ma," Peggy-Jean Ruth yelled, "ye jest called Sister Cecile a child."

"She aint a child, she's a growed woman," Lily-May spoke up from where she sat on the bench back of the long dining table.

"I know," Ma told them, " yer sister is growed but she's still my child. You young'uns are gittin' so ye correct ever'thin thet is said 'round here."

 Aint Jidy nodded in agreement, " Ye know hit's th larnin' they git at school now a'days."

The next morning promptly at seven-thirty people began to arrive for the wedding ceremony. All of Sister Cecile's and Toady's friends showed up, with lots of neighbors and relatives. It was almost like the Big June Meeting, so many people came.

The house filled up, then the yard was full and then some men went out in the calf lot, setting on the fence like Jay Birds. Sitting on the porch steps, I was just in time to catch the tail-end of the conversation between the Preacher's wife and Missus Biggers.

"Do tell," Missus Biggers was saying, "Ive never in my life heard th' like."

"I'd tell ye more," Missus Homingjoh replied, "but as th' sayin'
goes, little pitchers have big ears."

I knew they wanted me to move off the porch, but I had just been
pushed out of Sister Cecile's room, and Aint Jidy'd run me out of
the kitchen, so I wasn't going to move again, even for the
Preacher's wife.

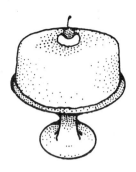

"Did ye see th' Bride's cake?" Missus Biggers asked, to change the subject.

"Yes, I did," Missus Homingjohn exclaimed, "I told some o' th' sisters that wuz in th' kitchen hit was th' pruttiest Bride' cake I ever laid my two open eye on."

"Yeh, hit shure is decorated prutty," Missus Biggers agreed.

"They tell me Mr. Pine's sister made hit, " Missus Homingjohn said, looking down where I was still sitting on the porch step.

"That's right, Aint Jidy shure did make hit," I spoke up.

"Did she, shure enough?" Missus Biggers asked.

"Yes siree, she seen th' picture in th' paper we put up on th' kitchen wall, an' hit told what t' put in hit," I wanted them to know all the details. "If ye want," I said getting up from the step, "I'll show you "x'actly where we found it."

I led the way to the kitchen, "here it is, right under th' picture about th' way t' keep young. Tells how to do the makin's and Aint Jidy figgered out th' rest lookin' at th' picture."

"Land sakes," Missus Biggers said, obviously impressed with Aint Jidy's skill. The Preacher's wife exclaimed about how Sister Cecile's cake looked "jest 'xactly" like that picture an' I for one cain't imagine how yer Aint Jidy did it"

"Ever' one cum t' Ma's room," Amy ran in to tell us, " 'th wedding' is gon'ter start right away."

I followed the women folk into Ma's room where Sister Cecile and Toady were standing by side. People kept crowding into the room and when there wasn't space for anymore. Folks were standing at the window and just outside both doors, and five or six were sitting Ma's bed. Every straight chair and rocker in the house was filled.

Preacher Homingjohn stood in the middle of the room facing the
bridal couple. Toady was wearing a black suit and a white shirt
buttoned to his neck. Sister Cecile wore her new dress and while it
was not "exactly" like the picture, it was, all agreed, "mighty
pretty." Ma was all smiles, since Sister Cecile had American
Beauty roses blossoming all over her dress, just like she'd told Ma
she wanted.

The L'il Man in the Machine

Granny Litton Pine, Pa's and Aint Jidy's Ma, lived in the hollow next to ours, in a log cabin built by her first husband. She told everyone she had "wore out five husbands," including my Pa's pappy, who died before I was born. Her third husband, Aint Jidy's Pa, "up an' left one day," leaving Granny Litton to raise her children all alone.

It was hard to tell Granny Litton's age, she was so shrivelled and dried up she looked like one of Ma's 'leather-britches.' But everyone who knew Granny Litton knew she was "strong as an ox" and she claimed the corn-cob pipe she had smoked since she was seven years old was the reason she was "right spry fer an' ol' woman."

When she came to visit us on one of her weekly trips, Granny
Litton liked best of all to sit on the porch, smoke her pipe and talk
with "th' young'uns." A cloud of blue smoke always seemed to
hang over her and I couldn't remember seeing Granny without her
cob pipe and leather tobacco pouch.

One Saturday morning Granny arrived with exciting news. Her neighbor, Isaac Perry, she said, had told her about a man who had come to Echo City with a "Vital Graph" machine he'd brought with him that he was showing to a lot of folks in town. Granny Litton said, while she didn't know exactly what it was, Isaac said a "Vital Graph" was a " new-fangled light machine with a crank on one side." When the machine was "cranked up," he told her, a little man would appear and, Granny said, you could watch him jump up and down to "beat all."

Pa said something so new and unusual deserved a look-see so we'd all best go have a look. Ma told him she had two dozen eggs and an old hen she could swap to get us in to see the man and his machine, so it was decided everyone would go into Echo City.

Aint Jidy, however, said she was "feelin porely" and, much as she'd like to see the little man, she thought she'd better stay home. She reckoned it was day-old roast duck she'd eaten that "wuzn't settin' well and had tied her "stumick in an end-all knot.".

She told us not to worry about her, though, for she was sure by the time we returned, she'd be feeling fine. So Pa hitched up the wagon and, telling Aint Jidy good-bye, we rode into Echo City.

The man and his machine, Granny said, were at the Hoskins' Feed and Produce Warehouse. Sure enough, a good-sized crowd had gathered and we could see a large white and green sign tacked up on the door which read, " See the world-renowned MPPC VitaGraph Show Here! Shows on the hour!".

Ma got out of the wagon with her hen tucked under one arm and a bucket of eggs in her other hand, went off to see if Missus Hoskins would take a laying hen and two dozen brown eggs as payment to let us in to see the Vita Graph show." She returned smiling so we knew we could go in.

Inside the feed store, someone had white-washed one wall and turned up fruit boxes for everyone to sit on. A tall, pale stranger was talking with several young ladies who lived right in Echo City. They had donned pretty frocks for the affair and seemed to laugh at everything the stranger said..

At first I thought they were laughing at the funny-looking cap which the man wore. He seemed not to know it had slipped down sideways on his head.. I later heard one of the town girls tell another that the man was wearing a very fashionable "berry" cap like those worn by lots and lots of folks in France.

After Missus Hoskins had collected admission fees and various bartered goods from all those who had come to see the man and his machine, Mr. Hoskins asked everyone to sit down. The girls all got to sit on boxes at the very front which had cushions on them, and the man in the berry hat told Mr. Hoskins to "pull the lights."

We sat in the dark waiting. Suddenly, on the white-washed store wall, a funny little man appeared, just like Granny had said. Several people in the audience cheered and clapped their hands but before long they were yelling for him to "watch out," for he was tottering on a roof top and in danger of falling.

As the man in the berry hat continued cranking his machine, the little man leaped off the roof top and ran down railroad tracks with a train almost upon him. Now the crowd really became excited and everyone yelled and screamed to warn the little man, but then, just at the last instant, he scampered out of the way of the train and ran into an alley.

Stumbling about, the funny little man had no end of near mishaps until he met a pretty young girl who took him by the arm and led him off. As they walked away, the lights went out and we sat in the dark once again.

Then, a voice in the darkness that I knew was Granny's, exclaimed, "well, sir hit's jest like Isaac was a'tellin' me, an' thet man in th' Vital Machine wuz carrying on like he'd had one too many."

With the show over all too soon, we got back onto the wagon and headed down the road home. We couldn't stop talking about the "new-fangled pictures thet move," and Granny Litton said it was a shame Aint Jidy had missed such an amazing sight, but no doubt we would tell her all about it, and the next time the man came to town, Aint Jidy could go.

As the horses stopped at the front gate, all of us young 'uns jumped down from the wagon and raced to find Aint Jidy. She was rocking contentedly on the front porch. "Well, folks, I visited th' outhouse three times while ye were gone an' I'm here t' tell ye I'm feelin' a sight better."

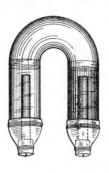

We took turns telling Aint Jidy about the little man who appeared on the wall, and Granny Litton said, "Jid, iffen I hadn't gone thar an' seen hit with my own two eyes, ye cudn't git me to b'lieve hit. There wuz this quare li'l man who come up outta thet machine an' he commenced prancin' around like he had ants in his drawers."

"Wuz he a dwarf?" Aint Jidy wanted to know.

"No," Granny Litton replied, "he warn't no dwarf, he jist 'ppeared t' me t' be stunted, and he waddled 'round like a duck thet'd been stepped on by a hoss."

"Ye know," Aint Jidy said with a little laugh," mebbe thet wuz whut wuz ailin' with thet duck leg I ate yestiddy."

Granny took her corncob pipe out of her apron pocket, and filled it with a twist of her favorite cut tobacco. Lighting her pipe she said with a contented sigh, "Well, ye kin tell all yer folks, thet ye heerd hit direct from me, Granny Litton, thet I kin die happy now, 'cause I've done seen hit all."

Plucks, Cracks and Fatback

When the days began growing colder and shorter, we knew it wouldn't be long until we'd have fresh meat on the table again. Although squirrels and possums were year-round fare and we had groundhogs and rabbits whenever Andrew went hunting, all of us surely looked forward to having "real meat"-- ham, sausage, chops and souse with nearly every meal.

Every last one of us Pines agreed there wasn't anything that could equal Ma's cornbread when it was made with fresh lard and "cracks" from just butchered hogs.

"Well, hits startin t' snow," Pa said one morning to no one in particular as he came in to warm himself by the cook stove. "Iffen hit gits colder an' th' moon turns right, we kin kill th' hogs, I reckon." Pa was never one to kill hogs on the day of a new moon, and while he knew of farmers who would kill their hogs

when the moon was "shrinking", Pa said no one in his right mind
would take them to market until the moon was "growing", since
this made the meat weigh more. Hearing butchering time was near,
Aint Jidy smacked her lips, rubbed her belly and said, "Be mighty
good t' have my insides greased up ag'in. I do b'lieve thet's whut's
been wrong with me, I need t' have a little hog grease in my
bellygut."

"Ye'r probably right," Ma agreed, "an' hit'll be good to git some good fresh plucks t' et, too." She went on, "Ye ever notice how th' plucks allus taste so good when ye first kill th' hogs?"

"I wouldn't doubt hit ary a bit iffen hit wuz 'cause ye hadn't had eny fer a while," Pa said, while blowing on his hands and rubbing them to get warm.

"Well, I luv th' meat but shurely hate all thet work thet hawg killin' brings on, " Aint Jidy stood with the back of her dress raised to the fire as she talked. "But once I git my belly full'a plucks I c'n work like a beaver."

"Seems like of late we don't have so much he'p," Ma complained, "when Peter an' Amy an' Sister Cecile wuz all here at home we could butcher five 'er six hogs in a day, an' git th' lard rendered out

an' th' sausage ground an' the guts cleaned an' just about ever' thin' else done up in one day."

"Well, hits th' truth they helped a heap," Pa agreed, "but ye gotta recollect they et a heap, too. 'Did ye stop t'think o' thet?"

"No-o," Ma shook her head decisively, "hit never once't crossed my mind. So I s'pose you an' Andrew will have t' kill th' hawgs agin this y'ar, same as ye done it last year."

"Well, th' young'uns kin stay home from school an' he'p," Pa said, "ever' blessed hand thet kin hold a knife or scrape a hog bristle will be thet much help."

That night it grew much colder. When Pa came in from the barn he said the thought of fresh meat had been too much for him and tomorrow would be "butchering day."

So we all went to bed early because we knew things would be astir long before daylight. When the clock in the parlor struck 'three', Ma arose and soon I could hear she had a fire blazing in the tin heater. When the room was good and warm, Pa got up. It was always Pa who called Aint Jidy out. Ma said Pa was the only one who could rouse Aint Jidy so she wouldn't "cum out of th' bed as cross as an old settin' hen."

45

Hearing Ma, Pa and Aint Jidy stirring about, Andrew and Woodrow Wilson came down from the loft where Ma had moved their bed since they had gotten so big. Pa and the boys went out into the cold to get out the old tar barrel Pa kept just for hog-scalding. Though it was bitter cold, there was enough moonlight so they could see to lean the barrel sideways over a stack of firewood, and before long they had a roaring fire going.

Pa told us to begin carrying buckets up from the stream to fill the barrel with water. I knew Pa had planned everything out so that by the time he and Andrew and Woodrow Wilson had eaten breakfast and sharpened all their knives on the grind-stone, the water in the barrel would be hot enough to scald the hogs, and there would be enough light for them to see.

We girls followed as Pa, Andrew and Woodrow Wilson went out to the pig pen. Pa took down one of the bars to the pen. By now it had gotten light enough we could see the big black hog that came out when Woodrow Wilson threw some corn on the ground. As the hog was busy rooting in the mud for the corn, Pa slipped up behind him, and, with the back of the ax he was holding, knocked the pig in the head. Pa got in a solid lick, hitting the black hog square on the head with a "thwack" right between the eyes.

The hog fell over instantly in a heap in the mud. Running up with a long-bladed knife, Andrew quickly slashed the hog's throat. Pa said Andrew had a "butcher's hand" for hog-killing, and he always seemed to know just where to cut a pig's "goozle pipe" so it would die quickly. Its blood arced up in a bright red ribbon, and after grunting and kicking a few times, the hog lay still.

Hearing all the commotion in the chip-yard made the other hogs in the pen restless. Pa said` "Now they've smelled blood, hits gonna be hard t' fool 'em with corn ag'in, so'll jest have t' use some good slop t' get th' next one."

Woodrow Wilson nudged the still-bleeding hog with his foot and said, "Pa, he's a goner." Then, grabbing one hind leg while Andrew got the other, they dragged the pig over to the tar barrel, and with a great heave they tossed the pig into the barrel of boiling water. Then, just as quick, they hauled him out. As they struggled with the hog, the sun suddenly appeared over the tree line, as if it was a part of Pa's planning.

Soon, we could see well enough to start scraping the hair off the hog. Pa said you couldn't leave a hog in hot water too long or it

would "set" rather than loosen the bristles. As he and Andrew
dunked the hog again and again -- "sousinng him good an' proper"
Pa said -- we set to work in earnest, scraping and scrubbing until
we had gotten most of the hair off.

Once most of the bristles had been removed, Pa made a cut across each of the hog's hind legs and Andrew ran a gambrel stick just behind the exposed tendon.

With Andrew and Pa each holding one end of the gambrel stick they raised the hog up on the "hawg pole" which had been set up on two forked supports. Then Pa cut all around the hog's neck so it would finish bleeding. With his knife Andrew went over every inch of the hide, snipping off any bristles which we had missed. Pa went off to git a pail of slop and when he returned, we all stopped to watch as the next pig came snorting out.

Pa's axe swung again, the second hog fell over, the knives came out and the butchering process began all over again. After four hours of hard work, the sun had risen well above the cherry tree in the chip yard. Aint Jidy came out with our largest dish pan and told Andrew, "Put th' plucks in h'yar, an' then I kin git 'em ready t' cook."

"They're so clean, ye won't have t' wash thim thet much, " Pa told
to her as he handed her his pan which he had filled to over-flowing
with pig hearts, livers, lungs and kidneys.

"I reckon maybe I'd better rinse 'em anyway, " Aint Jidy told Ma as
she carried the heavy pan back into the kitchen. Ma was too busy
taking the fat off the intestines to answer Aint Jidy right away.

Always one to save everything she came across, Ma could discover more uses for things that to the rest of us didn't seem of much value. She saved every piece of string -- no matter how short -- that came on packages from the store. Then in the Winter she would tie all the bits and pieces together and make the string which she used to tie her "leather-breeches" dried green beans together.

Ma would use the cotton pokes that sugar came in to make baby shirts for Sister Cecile and other relatives when they had babies. At hog butchering time, we knew little would be wasted. Us young'us always said Ma would save a pig's squeal if she could think of a use for it

There was one thing Ma always saved from hog butchering (which we surely could have done without) and this was hog-guts. Even though the smell made you want to hold your breath, Ma used hog intesines.

Ma would see to it that each of us had a sharp knife with a keen point, and then we'd start slitting intestines open and shake out the smelly contents. Once we had gotten a piece clean, we'd toss it in a tub of water to be washed later.

It usually took only a few minutes before the tub of water smelled as bad as the intestines, and after an hour of work, the three of us, the tub of water and the "clean" guts all smelled the same.

While we said there wasn't any doubt this was the worst part of hog butchering, the truth is none of us girls wanted to be the one stabbing the old pig in it's "goozle." So, as we worked on our chore, we thought about how good everything was going to taste.

Being Pine young'uns, though, we never missed a chance to make the most of moments when we could find something funny to take our attention from our labors. Peggy-Jean Ruth found a gut packed solid with manure, and instead of slitting it open, she'd sat it down on the chopping stump and with both hands given the gut a quick squeeze.

The manure squirted out like a Roman rocket clear across the chip yard. We laughed and laughed at the sight, and before long we began trying to out-shoot one another and see who could make her

manure-laden gut squirt the fartherest.. As usual, Lily-May ran off to tattle on us, which brought Ma out scolding us, Peggy-Jean Ruth, you young'uns have bin foolin' 'round so ye kin jest finish cleanin' th' rest of th' guts by yoreselves. Lily-May is comin' with me t' turn th' sausage mill fer a spell an' rest me. I'm plumb tuckered to a fare-the-well!"

"How many times do we have t' wash th' guts?" I asked Ma. "How many have ye done already?" When I told her they had been rinsed three time, she said, "I reckon thet's good enough. Yer Aint Jidy will want some whole guts to stuff th' sausage in and ye kin carry what's left inside fer her to use."

Besides all the fresh meat, sausage, ham, chittlin's and other things we got from butchering, we knew during the coming winter months Ma would save scraps of hog rind and collect all the bones and leavings from the table. Then when the Spring thaws arrived, we would carry water to the ash hopper that sat out in the chip yard.

Ma and Aint Jidy showed us how to pour water on the wood ashes that had accumulated there and wait for the copper-colored stream that appeared at the dripper. This was how they made lye each year. But because our lye was "home-made" it was always of uncertain strength. To test it, Aint Jidy would take a long turkey feather and dip it three times in the lye bucket. If the feathers left the quill clean, then the lye was just the right strength. But if a few barbs clung to the quill, then we'd add a can of store-bought lye.

When all the meat scraps, rinds, bones, hog guts and lye were tossed together in the big, black kettle' and cooked over a slow fire, the last parts of the hog would shortly be turned into soap.

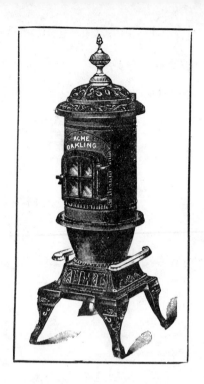

But at the moment none of us were thinking about washing up with soap, or even all the good things we would soon find on our dinner table.. Instead we were counting the hours and minutes until we would be finished with hog-butchering and could huddle around the big tin heater and warm ourselves.

The one thing we knew was that all of us would be "plumb tuckered out" from hauling, heating, scraping and cleaning hogs. To distract us, Peggy-Jean Ruth started talking about Christmas which we celebrated by bursting hog bladders saved from the butchering.

Pa had just come inside with a bladder and he spent the next few minutes preparing it. "Gimme a few more grains o' corn t' put into this 'un," Pa said, grunting with satisfaction as he blew into the hog bladder balloon and inflated it.

"Boy, I'm gonna be th' first to git up on Christmas mornin' an bust me a bladder, b'fore any one else," Woodrow Wilson declared. "No, ye ain't, neither," Pa said, "There's jist four hog bladders, so that's one fer Tom-Willie, an' one fer Lily-May an' one fer you an' one fer Peg-".

"I decided I don't want one this year, Pa", Peggy-Jean Ruth said. "Tom-Willie kin have mine."

"I don't want one neither," Lily-May chimed in, " Give mine to Woodrow Wilson."

Looking up, Pa asked,, "What's got in t' you gals? Sounds t' me like yer gittin too big t' bust hog bladders anymore"

"Yeh," they answered together, and the boys shouted, " that means we'll each git to bust two bladders for Christmas!"

"Well, here ye go," Pa said as he gave them to Tom-Willie and Woodrow Wilson, "hang 'em up on th' winder nail an' by Christmas they"ll be good an' dry an' likely pop louder than a clap o' summer thunder."

"I wish't they wuz dry now, " Tom-Willis said wistfully, taking them from Pa. "I'd shure like t' bust one right now under Aint Jidy's chur, jest t' see her jump. Th' way she's nodding her head an' snorin', she'd jump clean up t' th' sky!"

"Now doncha be mean t' yer Aint Jid, " Pa scolded him." She's got her belly full 'a plucks an' cracklin cornbread, so she's happier then a hoss in a field of fresh clover."

"Hit's a sight t' behold what she kin put away," Ma told him.

"You know how much o' that possum she et last Sunday?" Andrew asked in a near whisper for fear of waking her. "She ate th' whole of th' last one I kilt."

"I know she like t' made herself sick etin' all thet possum gravy an' taters," Ma agreed.

"She et a peck," Pa agreed with Andrew, "I sat right thar an' watched her go after both hind legs, th' back an' a fore paw, as well as most o' th' neck. Had possum grease a runnin' all over her face." Then, to himself, Pa said, "Yep, if there's one thin' I know fer sartain, its thet yer Aint Jid loves her vittles."

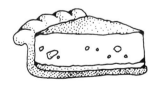

"Well," Ma said, "hits no wonder why she's puny. She nearly run herself t' death goin' t' th' backhouse fer two whole days after she et that possum. Hit didn't lay well on her stummick and she took might' near a whole new Roebuck catalog out thar with her. By th' time she wuz done trottin', she had gone plumb through the housewares an' wimmins' sections."

"Well, th' way she took out after them plucks t'day", Pa said with a chuckle, " my guess is she's in for some more trottin' an' I 'speck she'll be all th' way int' garden seeds an' farming tools!"

Our laughter woke Tom-Willie who had fallen asleep and he asked Ma if he could have something "speshul."

"What do ye want thet's special?" Ma asked him.

"Will ya save me th' hog's eyes, when you clean th' head?"

"What on earth fer?" Ma looked at him in surprise. Pigs' eyes were one thing she didn't save.

"I wanta put them in my hand an' close my eyes tight an' see if I kin see t' walk with th' hog eyes." Tom-Willie explained.

"No, ye kain't," Peggy-Jean Ruth told him, "th' hog's eyes are dead an nothin' can see after hits dead."

"Tell you what," Andrew said, smiling at Tom-Willie and winking to us girls,, "I'll pull a couple of them hog teeth out an' ye kin stick them in front of yer mouth where you just lost yers."

Knowing he was being teased, Tom-Wille climbed up into Ma's lap and hid his face. Andrew made a face at Tom-Willie and grinned at us girls.

Pa stretched, scratched himself and looked at the clock. With a long sigh, he said, "Somebody better wake up yer Aint Jidy so we kin all git t'bed," ending our long day "with the hogs.".

WATCH THE BIRDIE!

"Hey! Hey" Pa shouted as he came in from Echo City one afternoon. "Where's ever'body?" Hearing Pa, Ma and Aint Jidy both came running from different parts of the house to the front porch, for Pa had used his "come hyar now" voice, and there no telling what might have happened. In fact, he was standing

in the yard talking to a stranger. The stranger, a small little man in
a black suit sported a shiny black hat with a big white feather stuck
in the brim, and he had some contraption slung over his
shoulder. I could see that it had three long prongs stuck out in
front.

My first I thought was it might be some kind of post-hole digger,
but it had a fair-sized black box on one end so I knew it wasn't for
digging holes. Besides, Pa had a hole-digger, so I knew he
wouldn't have called all of us to come running just to see a new
hole digger.

Ma and Aint Jidy stopped dead in their tracks when they saw the stranger. Tom-Willie had gotten such a running start from the kitchen that when they stopped, he plowed straight into them. He landed top-side down on the porch at Pa's feet. Pa leaned down and, picking Tom-Willie up, set him on his feet.

Ma said, "What'cha want, Roger?"

"This hyar is a pitcher-takin' man," Pa told her, "I run int' him comin' from Echo City an' I recollect ye been sayin' as t' how you'd like t' have th' young'uns pitchers took. Yer allus sayin' they'll soon be scatter'd t' th' four winds an'--"

"You know as well as I do they ain't all hyar," Ma cut him off, " Sister Cecile's marr'd an' --"

"I know all thet," Pa nodded his head vigorously, then went on, "but I figger'd th' pitcher man could take th' pitcher o' th' young'uns who are still hyar, an' iffen ye don't want hit took, all's well an' done. But hit's hard t' tell when he'll be comin' this way agin."

All the time Pa was speaking, the stranger was bobbing his head up and down agreeing with everything Pa said.

"Might not git 'nuther chance like this'n in a month of Sunday's," Pa finished.

"Yep, I don' rightly know when I'll be 'round this way agin," the pitcher-takin' man looked even more concerned about our chances of never seeing him again.

Ma nodded her head at the wisdom of Pa's comments and she looked over, first at us young' uns, then at Pa, and then at the stranger. Then she said, "Ye jest gon'ter take th' pitcher only o' the young'uns?"

"No, no," Pa explained to her, "figger th' whole family could be took." At this Aint Jidy seemed to perk up, and Ma asked, "How much is hit gonter cost?"

"Fifty cents." The pitcher-takin' man obviously felt he had just given Ma a bargain price.
"Fifty cents! Jist fer one?" Ma gasped and, obviously, she felt his price was anything but a bargain. Aint Jidy said, "Heavenly Day!"

but I couldn't tell if she agreed with Ma, or if she thought the pitcher-takin' man's price was a big bargain.

"One won't be near' enough, but they're so high an' costly, we caint git but th' one, an' iffen we have jist th' one pitcher took, ever'body an' his brother'll be wantin' hit," Ma appeared to be talking to Aint Jidy but I knew she was saying this to talk the man out of his price. She sighed and sounded resigned to not having a picture made. Then she said, "an' iffen we did decide t' have more'n one made, I'd want one fer Peter, one fer Sister Cecile, one t' put in the Bible, another fer--"

"I can make as many as ye want, " the man tried to head her off. "Landsakes, no, ye, cain't," Ma argued back, "fer I aint got no money t' pay ye fer even one at the price ye want."

Pa had remained silent until now but then he removed his battered straw hat and scratched the thinning patch in his hair. Cocking one eye and tilting his head a little, he said, "Might ye make a trade fer th' pitchers thet Phoebe wants?."

"Whatcha got in mind?" Althought the pitcher-takin' man tried not to sound too interested in Pa's question, the words fairly flew out of his mouth.

Smelling a possible deal, Pa looked side-ways at Ma and said,

"Phoebe, count up how many pitchers ye' want an' then I'll know what t' offer."

"Well, now, less see," Ma began, "one for Peter--"
"Hit'll please his soul plumb t' death, bless his heart, t' git a family pitcher o' us all, " Aint Jidy interupted eagerly.
"One fer Sister Cecile." Ma began again, "an' one fer my Ma, an' Sister Susie' ll want one, an' --"
"I'd like awful well t' have one fer me," Aint Jidy interupted Ma a second time.

"Yes, one fer Aint Jidy hyar," Ma motioned toward her, "an I want one t' put aside in th' trunk t' keep fer me an' you, " Ma looked at Pa who seemed to be agreeing we would need a considerable number.

"Anybody else ye can think o' thet would want er need one?" The pitcher-takin' man asked.

"No, I reckon tha'ss about hit," Ma told him.
"How many d'ya figger she wants?" Pa wanted to know, looking at the man..

"Six," the picture-takin' man replied after he had ticked them off on his fingers.
"Ye shure?" Pa asked, not trusting the man's counting, and moving his lips silently as he counted: Peter, Sister Cecile, Phoebe's Ma, Phoebe's sister Susie, an' Aint Jidy."

He closed his hand to show that he was five, then he raised the forefinger of his left hand, "An' one fer us, " he said aloud.

"You wuz right about how many we need," he told the man.

"Fifty-cents a pitcher makes," Ma paused and did some calculating on her fingers.

"Hit'll be jest three dollars even, " the man told her as if this were a "piddlin'" sum and a bargain not to be missed.

"Landsakes!" Ma exclaimed again, this time the tone in her voice signalled that three dollars was not a bargain the picture-taking man said it was,

Pa, meantime, had counted again on his fingers and declared that six was the" right figger."

"So, d'ya want th' pictures struck 'er dontcha?" the man asked, not waiting for an answer but starting to open up the camera legs.

"Will ye trade?" Pa asked with an eye-brow raised.
"What'cha willin' to trade? the man tried to match Pa's unconcerned tone and look of disinterest..

"How 'bout a ham o' meat," Pa asked, ready to negotiate if he had to, "would ye swap fer that?"

"How much is hit a pound?" Now the pitcher-takin' man removed his hat and scratched the back of his head.
"Ten cents," Pa declared promptly, and added, " I jest t'day asked, fer curiosity's sake, while I was in t' Echo City. Like t' keep up with th' prices o' meat an' things."

"How much will yer ham weigh?" The man looked at Pa. Pa looked at Ma and Ma looked at the pitcher-taking man.
"Hit'll weigh at least forty pounds," Ma spoke up before Pa had a chance.
"Wudn't doubt hit a bit," Pa said, confirming her estimate, "specially thet big ham thet cum frum the hind quarters o' th' ol' sow."

"Vangie," Aint Jidy called me and handed me the water-bucket saying, "Run t' th' spring an' fetch up a buchet o' water. I gotta git my neck an' face warshed an my head combed fer th' man t' take my pitcher."

The man scarcely paused before he said, "I'll trade ye that'ta way." And he sat up the picture-taking contraption on its three legs while we all watched with great curiosity.

"Git th' young'uns all t'gether, " Pa told us.
"Lily-May, " Ma called from the end of the porch.
"Peg-gie-eee Jee-ann R-uuu-th, " Aint Jidy's voice whined like a fiddle string pulled too tight.

"Tom-Willie," Pa said, "run find Andrew and Woodrow Wilson an' tell 'em t' git over hyar right now."
"They went clean t' th' back pasture early this morning t' fix the

fence gate," Ma told him.

"Hyar, have a chur," Pa told the man, "hit won't take long t' round 'em all up."

I was too excited about the picture taking to voice my usual complaints about carryung water from the spring house. Aint Jidy washed her face with great care, then she took a cloth and cleaned the wax from her ears. Next she slushed water mixed with a teaspoonful of salt around in her mouth. After this, she combed her hair and then got out her Sunday-Go-to-Meeting black poplin dress with the white lace collar.

When she was done, she pinned her sweetheart brooch securely at her throat. Seeing her in her Sunday finery during the week made Aint Jidy look kind of special. If it hadn't been for her size ten feet -- Pa said the Lorddidn't jist hand out feet to Aint Jid, He turned her legs under -- she would have looked as fine as a new penny.

Pa's remarks never didn't bother Aint Jidy, just as his frequent comments that someday she'd meet a man and make a fine wife. Watching her get ready for the picture taking reminded me of just how different she was from Ma, who, having removed her sun bonnet, had run her fingers through her hair, and announced she was "all set" to have her picture struck..

Tom-Willie soon returned with Andrew and Woodrow Wilson and Pa said we were ready. The boys didn't bother to put on clean

overalls but Ma made them change their shirts. Andrew's overalls, she said, were "as dirty as sin" and Woodrow Wilson had torn a big hole in the seat of his pants when he crawled under the wire fence a Sunday back.

When at last we assembled on the porch, the pitcher-takin' man picked up a straight-back chair and asked Andrew and Woodrow Wilson to fetch two more and follow him. They took the chairs to the sunny side of the house and set them in a row.

He had Pa set in the middle chair, with Ma and Aint Jidy on either side. Pa squirmed and looked like something was itching him where he couldn't reach. It struck me that this was one of the few times I had seen Pa set in anything but the porch rocker.
"Does hit make a heap o' difference whut kind o' chur ye have in the pitcher?" Pa asked.

"No, so long as ever'one sets up straight," the man replied as he tried to get us lined up in order.
"Andrew," Pa jumped up out of the straight chair as he spoke, "go fetch me out my ol' rocker."

Ma plumped up the duck feather pillows in Pa's rocker when Andrew brought it from the porch, and Pa sank down contented. When he, Ma and Aint Jidy were finally settled in their places, the pitcher-takin' man posed Tom-Willie between Pa's legs. Then Ma said she'd rather have him set on her lap, since he was the baby of the family.

The pitcher-takin' man had Peggy-Jean Ruth stand by Aint Jidy and Aint Jidy said she thought it would look real pretty if Peggy-Jean Ruth would place her hand lightly on Aint Jidy's shoulder. Then the man asked Andrew and Woodrow Wilson to stand just back of Pa. I stood by Andrew, Lily-May took her place next to Woodrow Wilson, and Amy stood next to her.

"Is this all o' yer clan?" the man asked finally.

"Yep," Pa answered, " this is all that's still on the farm."

"Course, we have Sister Cecile Stumpgate down th' road a piece an'..." Ma began.

"Yes, you done told me about them," the man interupted her before she could finish.

Ma leaned over to Pa and, covering her mouth with her hand, muttered, "Don'cha think hit'd be kinda nice iffen he'd let us set two empty straight chairs, jest t' show we got two more?"

"No-o-o," Pa told her, "it might not look right t' have two empty churs in th' pitcher, folks might think they wuz dead, 'er somethin'? "Never thought o' hit thataway, " Ma relented, " so I reckon we'll jest have t' tell ever'one who's missin'."

After several minutes of adjusting his camera, the picture-taking man said he was ready. He told us to "look our best", but then he stopped and asked Pa if he would like to look through the lens to see if we looked alright to him. So Pa went over to the camera and the man adjusted the black hood over Pa's head.

We thought Pa looked funny with the black hood over his head, and started laughing but Ma gave us her hawkeye so we stopped as quick as we started. When Pa returned to his rocker, Ma asked, "How'd we all look?"
"Jest like ye do now, clear as day," Pa answered.

"Wonder iffen he'd let me look through," Ma whispered excitedly to Pa, "I've never looked through one o' thim things afore."

"Can Phoebe look through thet thing?" Pa asked the man who was back under the hood again.

"Sure, let her have a look-see," he said, holding the cloth up for her

and waiting.   Ma came back to her place, she whispered to Aint
Jidy, "Hit's a sight t ook through one o' thim things. I'd give a
pretty iffen ye could jest see."
"Wait! Wait!" Aint Jidy screamed wildly, leaping to her feet.
""Whut's wrong with ye, Jid?" Pa wanted to know.
"I wanta look through that contraption," Aint Jidy exclaimed and
said, "I'm gittin' up in years an' there's no tellin' iffen I will live t'
see another one o' thim things." She might have been on the verge
of tears as she looked first at Pa and then the picture-taking man.

Hearing and seeing Aint Jidy's agitation, the pitcher-takin' man
popped out from under his hood, removed his glasses and pinched
the bridge of his nose. Pa said, " Ye reckon, kin my sister, Jidy--"

"Yes, yes," the man said, with a sigh, " let her have a look, too."

Aint Jidy, trembling and looking like she thought there might be a snake under the black hood, went to take a look through the camera lens. She returned with her face lit up by a big smile, and the man sighed once more and said, "might as well have yer young'uns have a look, too."

Ma carried Tom-Willie and held him up to have the first look. Then one by one we went to look through. I didn't see much as it was dark beneath the black cloth and I kept my eyes shut tight. Andrew was the last to look, and when he returned to his place, the man asked, "Ever'body ready now?"

"Yes," Pa assured him and we all tried to smile without fidgeting.

85

Suddenly, the man yelled out, "watch the birdie!" and everyone's head swiveled toward the cherry tree in the chip yard.

It took two more times before the pitcher-takin' man said, "All done." He quickly folded his camera, shook hands with Pa, told everyone good-day and left.

Two weeks later to the day, the pitcher-takin' man returned with our pictures. Pa gave him the ham of meat wrapped in a flour sack and Ma got a dollar " to boot" from the picture-man, to make up

the difference between the ham and the pictures.   After he left with

the ham, we all agreed Ma once again had struck a real bargain.

We gathered around her to see the pictures and we all said it was

surely a sight to behold-- ever' last one of us looked just like our

pictures!.

Ballard's Best Goes to School

The days following the Big June Meeting were long, sweltering-hot and a time when Pa worked all of us young'uns pretty hard. We hardly had time to marvel at the colors of the summer although red tomatoes, green peppers and yellow squash appeared daily at our dinner table. It seemed to take forever before the sweet odor of new mown hay signaled the end of our summer of hard work.

After a week of "pitchin' hay" us young'uns ached each year for the start of school which would let us escape the worst of our farm chores. Older children went to the city school where they had to pay a tuition fee. Peter, Amy and Sister Cecile didn't go to school any more. Pa said, " I jest ain't got th' money fer sech foolishness." Tom-Willie didn't go to school, either. He wasn't old enough, and, anyway, as Ma said, "he still nu'sin'".

Every morning during the week, there was a rush to get everyone who was going off to school fixed up with a paper poke full of victuals. This meant Peggy-Jean Ruth, Woodrow Wilson, Lily-May, Andrew and me each had a poke to take to school for our lunch.

Aint Jidy wouldn't let anyone but herself pack Andrew's lunch. We all knew he was her special pick of the Pines. Before she'd eat a bite at the breakfast table, she'd set aside the best pieces of streaked meat and her prettiest biscuits with a hard-fried egg, the way he liked them.

Then after she ate, she'd fix his poke, and nearly always she'd slip in a jam and butter biscuit extra. We didn't mind Aint Jidy being partial, for the truth was that we all got pretty much the same fare in our pokes.

I loved school, or rather would have loved school, had it not been for some bullies who let us know they thought they were better than us Pines. There were also some students from the City who had pretty store-bought dresses and carried their lunches in little reed baskets. They made fun of my clothes, and said I wore chop-sack drawers that still had flour in them.

While they made life miserable, I mostly let on like I didn't hear them. It would have been a lot worse had they discovered that all of us Pines wore chop-sack drawers. Ma had a favorite pattern for cutting out our drawers. Taking the sacks the cow feed came in, she'd cut a hole in each corner for the legs. Then she'd stitch wide hem in the open end of the sack, and run a draw-string through it to gather the top

Sometimes she'd use a feed sack and make a petticoat from it, so some of us girls could have "matching" drawers and petticoats. .

Pa wore the drawers made for him all summer but with the first

frost he took them off and climbed into one of the two pairs of store-boughten red flannels Ma got him each year.

I sometimes thought about telling the other children about Pa's store-bought clothes, but was afraid they would tease me.

Unlike Pa, us girls wore our chopsack garments year-round. On a windy day, we worried that the wind would raise our dresses and everyone would read, "Ballard's Best" plain as anything on our backsides. The home-made lye Ma used to bleach the sacks was never strong enough to get the red letters out. so we lived in fear of being found out and being teased as a "Ballard's Best" girl.

One day in Miss Adrianna Barksdale's fourth grade class, I was chosen to select a poem and recite it from memory before the entire school.   Ma helped me find some verses and I learned my lines soon enough. What to wear was my chief concern. I thought about getting "sick" as a way out of having to appear in my hand-me-down clothes in front of all the students. Ma proposed I dress up in a pair of Andrew's overalls, along with one of Pa's battered old hats, so the children in school could see I was in a "costume.".

The day of the recital I told Ma and Aint Jidy I really was sick. Since I half-believed it myself it wasn't hard to screw up my face and fall back into bed, to convince everyone I wasn't "faking". Aint Jidy, however, said I had such good color in my cheeks it mustn't be anything serious. Ma got me out of bed, dressed and out the door before I could plead one last time, so I set out for school repeating the lines of poem over and over to myself.

When the time came for the school assembly I was certain everyone would see my knees knocking together, even though Andrew's overalls were four sizes too big for me. Miss Barksdale called my name and said, "Now Evangeline Pine is going to recite from memory, a poem she has selected, which she tells me is entitled , "The Railroad Crossing".

I took a deep breath, shut my eyes and began"

"I started down to Davy Jones with that there team of mine
A-hauling down a load of corn to Ebberneezer Cline
I was driving slow fer jest about a day or so,
Cause the off horse stuck a splinter in his foot and made it sore.

You know the railroad cuts across the road at Martin's Hole
Well, there I seed a great big sign risin' high upon a pole
I thought I'd stop an' read the thing an' find out what it said,
So I stopped the hosses on the railroad track and read.

I ain't no scholar, recollect, an' so I had t' spell. I started

95

*kinda cautious-like, with "R-A-I-L. That was "rail." :R-O-
A-D spelled "Road. "Railroad. The C-R-O-S-S-I-N-G
made it "railroad crossing."*
L-O-O-K was "look", O-U-T was "out." and f-o-r was "for"

I got that far when suddenly there came an awful whack.
A thousand fire-y thunderbolts jest scooted me off the track.

The hosses went to Davy Jones, The wagon went to smash.
An' I was heisted seven miles above the tallest ash.
I didn't come to life agin fer 'bout a day or two

An' though I'm crippled up a heap I've sorta struggled through

*It ain't the pain, an' it ain't the loss of that 'er team of mine
But, stranger, I'd like to know... WHAT was the rest of that there sign?"*

Finishing with a flourish, I curtsied and sat down to the sound of much applause and laughter. Several students from Echo City came up to tell me they really liked the poem -- and my costume! After that I wasn't teased any longer about wearing chopsack drawers, and I mostly agreed with Ma when she told me, "there aint thet many girls in yer school who git t'have sech a nice label on their bloomers!"

THE WRITING ON THE KITCHEN WALL

The best thing about Spring Cleaning each year was helping Ma put up new paper on the kitchen walls. One day in early April Ma said, "Vangie, ye an' Lily-May go t' Echo City an' beg fer some newspapers an' order books an' seed catalogs. They allus have pretty pictures in thim, an' hit'll do a world of good fer me t' paste them up in th' kitchen. I declare th' smoke this past winter has been somethin' t' put up with, an' hits turned th' walls almost black!"

Tucking the sacks Ma gave us under our arms, Lily-May and I sat out down the road to Echo City. A trip into town was a favorite adventure and we both looked forward to errands which took us to'the big city." We always got to see so many people bustling about and it seemed they were always eager to get to someplace other than where they were. Also, I liked to look in the store windows and see glass show cases full of hard candies. I never tired of imagining how the big, striped peppermint sticks would

taste when I first put them in my mouth, and I could even imagine
how it would be to have my fill of sweets.

There were always other, "secret" things to draw my attention. At
Weaver Brothers General Store I stopped to admire the bright bolts
of dress cloth displayed in the window. I pictured myself in a
pretty dress made from some purple-flowered material, and in my
mind's eye I added a straw hat I had seen in the ready-to-wear store
next door.

Lily-May didn't much care about clothes but was more interested
in the fancy houses city folk lived in. As we walked along that
morning, we agreed I should do the begging for the papers since I
could whine through my nose better than she could.
"Vangie," Lily-May told me with a sigh, "next t' Peggy-Jean Ruth

you can whine better'n anyone I ever heard."

Pleased with the compliment but not wanting to miss an opportunity to complain, I said, "I don't see why Ma don't make Peggy-Jean Ruth come an' beg fer paper, since she's such a good whiner. I bet you an' Peggy-Jean Ruth could have gotten more than enough t' paste up in th' kitchen. It's jist not fair that I have t' do hit

all!" This last complaint let me practice my nasal whine with the right look of resignation.

We'd reached a row of big, white houses by this time and Lily-May suggested we go up to the imposing house on the corner that had an ornate iron fence running all around. We went to the door and knocked. When the door opened, I asked the lady who confronted us, "Do ye have any ol' newspapers 'er order books 'er seed catalogs t' give away?"

Her answer took us by surprise, "Yes, little girl, as a matter of fact I think I have quite a few." She didn't seem one bit surprised at my question, so, screwing up my courage, I said, "Would ye have any ol' clothes, 'er maybe some lightbread sandwiches?" I held my breath and gave Lily-May a look that told her she'd better not spoil

our chances.

"I'll see what I can find,: the lady smiled again and left us standing
on the porch.

"Vangie Pine," Lily-May whispered, "Ma'll skin ye alive an' take
all th' hide offen yer behind when I tell her ye begged fer som'thing'
t' eat." Her eyes were open wide at the thought of Ma discovering

what I had done. She went on, "but I AM hungry right this minute
an' a sandwich or biscuit shure would taste good."

"Me, too," I told her, "so we might as well see what we kin git.
You DID say I whine good."

"An' iffen ye say a word t' Ma, I'll beat ye black and blue," and I
pinched her arm quick just to give her an idea. Lily-May didn't
have a chance to yell because just then the lady came back with a

paper poke and an assortment of newspapers, order books and a seed catalog. She went back inside and this time came out with her arms full of clothes. I'd never before seen so many store-bought clothes and Lily-May and I looked at one another in dis-belief.

Thanking the lady repeatedly, we staggered away with our loads. As we reached the corner crossing we decided we had done so well with just one try we might as well head back home. As soon as we had passed the last clap board dwellings in Echo City we sat down by the side of the road and quickly ate the two whitebread sandwiches we found in the poke.

To our delight we discovered two oatmeal cookies which had both raisins and nuts. We could scarcely believe our good fortune and lost no time in gobbling up the sandwiches and cookies.

Once our stomachs were full, we could see we would need more papers. So, leaving Lily-May to guard our things, I returned to town to beg out more order books and papers. Before long I had my arms full of newspapers, several ladies' magazines and a nice flower-seed catalog.

Lily-May sat on the side of the road waiting for me and as we trudged home I began to go over in my mind what I was going to tell Ma. In all the times we had been sent out to collect paper to paste up on the kitchen walls, none of us had ever begged for food or clothes. Ma's reaction, I was sure, was not one I would like.

Luckily, Aint Jidy met us at the door, "Wull, I s'wan, hit looks like ye done right well with yer beggin'," she said approvingly.
"Yeh, we done alright, I reckon," I replied, trying to sound all the while like there was nothing unusual about all the things we had returned with.
Coming from the kitchen, Ma exclaimed,. "Whoo-pee! where did ye git all o' thim clothes, Vangie?"
"Th' woman in th' very first house we went up to wanted t' give them to Lily-May and me," I said, thinking, while I didn't want to share any praise or rewards, it might we wise to include Lily-May and spread any punishment .

"Did ye git anythin' else?" Aint Jidy, obviously more interested in seeing what things were in our biggest bags, appeared unconcerned about our begging.

"They gived us two lightbread sandwichs and two whole oat-meal cookies with raisins an' nuts!" Lily-May answered excitedly before I could shut her up.
"Why that wuz real nice o' thet lady," Ma said, and I took my first deep breath of the afternoon.

After supper we cleared up as fast we could with everybody helping, then we piled the clothes, papers and catalogs on the table. Ma sorted through the bag of clothes, and she and Aint Jidy held up each garment up for inspection.

Once the clothes were divided up among all us girls, we spent the rest of the evening catching up on a year of news and fashions. We set aside favorite scenes and pictures of pretty dresses from the magazines to paste up on the kitchen wall, and Pa said , since there wasn't much to do on the farm, so we could help paper the kitchen.

Early the next morning Ma made up a kettle of flour paste and we set to work. This was as good as, or even better than the Fourth of July? We got to look through all the catalogs, pick out dresses we especially liked, and paste up our favorite scenes on the wall just behind the kitchen table.

I was dreaming about how I would look with one of the new, "bobbed" hair-do's when Aint Jidy scolded in a loud, exasperated voice, "Peggy-Jean Ruth, ye have all of th' women pasted upside down!" Sure enough, she had three pictures pasted up wrong.

"Th' blood'll all run their heads!" she wailed, "hit'll kill 'em," and tears began to roll down her cheeks.
"No, chil', not iffen ye'll jest paste anuther pitcher over thim," Aint

Jidy tried to calm Peggy-Jean Ruth by handing her a piece of paper.

"Now here's a pretty pitcher o' red roses. Put hit over thim. See, that's jest as nice as kin be."

Aint Jidy stepped back and surveyed the repairs. "Iffen we had us some strips o' wood t' make a square fer hit, this would exactly like a framed pitcher from th' store."

"Ma, look at this," Amy called out, 'here's a really pretty dress an' hits only $2.98." and she commenced to read the description: "a frock with lovely lines and American Beauty roses flowering in large print on the puff sleeves and full skirt. Price includes a pretty Basque waist set wide set in with a band belt."

"Kin I send off fer hit?" Amy pleaded.

"D' ye think they might take eggs n' butter fer hit?" Ma asked her.

"I aint sure," Amy replied, "hit says t' send cash or money order."

"In that case, ye cain't git hit, " Ma told her," besides that's jest too much fer anyone t' pay fer one dress! Why, fer $2.98 I could go to Echo City an' buy enough print t' make ever' one of you young'uns a dress with enough left over fer Tom-Willie to git a short-sleeve shirt."

That evening when Pa came in from the fields, he went right away to survey the new paper on the kitchen wall. "Hit shure looks nice

'n clean," he declared, and he set about looking at all the pictures and articles of interest which we had put up on the walls.

"Iffen hit would jest stay that'away, hit'd be prutty," Ma answered, "but ever' blessed summer th' flies jest speck th' paper, and then, in

th' winter th' stove smokes up what the flies haven't ruin't, and when Spring comes 'round, this kitchen is a sight t' behold."

"Flies don't bother me none," Pa said, "an I allus been told hit wuz healthy iffen th' flies stayed 'round. Sort of a sign of good things to eat."

"Thet reminds me," Ma turned to Lily-May, "run git me a fly-bush offen th' tree by th' spring."

"Make Vangie, she' tallern' me." Lily-May did a good imitation of me whining.

"Well, go tell her," Ma said, not concerned about who did

something as long as it got done. Especially when she was concentrated on her cooking, Ma left all the squabbling to us.

"Vangie, Vangie-e-e" Lily-May started shouting, "Ma said fer ye t' go an' git her a fly-bush!"

"Now, I heered ever' last word that wuz said," I spoke from where I sat on my favorite perch on the porch steps, " an' ye kin jest git yerself out there an git th' flybush offen the tree."
I knew Ma wanted the flybush so when we ate dinner and if I waited, Lily-May would have to go.

Shortly Aint Jidy called us to eat and we all said how nice the kitchen looked with its new papering. Re-doing the walls always seemed to inspire Ma's cooking and she had hog's jaw, wild dandelion salad and buttermilk cornbread.

Every few minutes Ma would pick up the fly bush and swing it over our heads.

"Phoebe, I declare, I'd druther have th' flies et with me than put up with that thing swishin' like a hoss's tail flappin' over me," Pa complained as Ma continued to shoo flies from the table.

"Ma, kin I make a fly bush like Aint Susie made?" Amy asked.
Before Ma could answer, Aint Jidy spoke up, "No, ye cain't. What

paper's left over is gon'ter go fer th' backhouse. Thim cobs is jest too rough fer me."

Aint Jidy's remark brought a smile to Pa's face, "they are sorta rough t' use," he agreed with Aint Jidy, "an' it allus seems like we run short o' paper. But this time, I think th' young'un got enough t' keep th' backhouse in paper and fer Amy to have some to make a fly bush with."

Then he told her, "I'll tell ye whut, I'll jest nail up an ol' hemp sack inside the backhouse door, then ye kin jest give a swipe as ye come out."

Pa found this notion particularly funny, and he had a good laugh before adding, "thet a'way he won't need cobs nor paper neither."

"Roger Pine," Ma fixed him with her most ferocious hawkeye, "ye'd better bridle yer tongue right this instant!" Pa looked a bit sheepish, as Ma went on, "An' anuther thin' while we're talkin' about the backhouse an' cobs, I wish ye'd save th' nice clean red cobs fer syrup. Th' young' uns likes hit powerful good."

"Whyn't ye go out t' th' backhouse an' git th' red cobs outta th' cob box?" Pa wanted to know.

"Hit sets right thar in th' corner."

"After ye put thim in th' backhouse, they don't seem clean no more, " Ma complained.

"Clean!" Pa erupted, "there ain't no difference a'tall between eatin' syrup made from cobs from th' backhouse than etin' pickled hog snouts after th' hog roots his rooter 'round a cow pile all day."

"Roger Washington Pine," Ma's response was a signal that Pa was in trouble, "ye've said too much, so jest hush up."

"An' at the dinner-table, too," Aint Jidy chimed in and looked at him disapprovingly.

"Well, hits the Gospel truth. There ain't no difference," Pa wasn't going to give up so easily and we knew he couldn't be hushed up so easily. We also knew Aint Jidy. She looked at him with her head balanced primly on top of the high white rolled collar she always wore.

Aint Jidy looked just like an angry little hen in the chipyard glaring at some rooster who had caused a ruckus. But once we started to laugh at what Pa said, it seemed we couldn't stop. Ma's protests and Aint Jidy's appearance just made us laugh all the more.

"Hit does a body good t'have a hearty laugh after sech a fine meal, I do believe," Pa said by way of an apology. Ma sighed and Aint Jidy harrumphed as they began clearing the dishes from the table.

"What's thet yer' readin', Peter," Pa asked. We all turned to look where Peter was reading from the kitchen wall.

"Listen t' this," Peter said, and he commenced to read: "Wanted by fertilizer manufacturer doing national business. Field representatives to represent the Company in the Western states, handling sales and collections. Familiarity with territory desirable but not essential. This industry is offering permanent positions to the right parties with rapid advancement for able-bodied men. Come West young men and seek your fortune! For further information write:

Thomas & Thomas Fertilizer Co. Box 4334 Dept. C. San Francisco, California."

When Peter had finished reading, Aint Jidy asked, "Don't it tell how much they pay?"

"No, but I aim to write this Thomas & Thomas an' ask him."

"I knowed ye aint been satisfied livin' hyar since ye got growed up," Pa admitted with a sigh, "but I never fer a minute ever thought ye'd want to go so far away."

"How'd ye know how I felt?" Peter wanted to know what Pa meant.

Ma interupted, saying, "I kin tell ye. Ye don't take no notice a'tall o' any 'o th' girls here 'bout. Most boys yore age has already got thim a woman an' two er three young'uns."

Peter was quiet as Pa responded, "I allus heerd Californey is a right purty country," and after a long, contemplative pause, he went on, " they say it stays warm there th' year 'round."

"Well, I might go," Peter said, "iffen fer nothin' else but jest t' look 'round. I ain't never been nowhere but West Virginny Kaintuck an' Tennessee."

Another long pause showed Pa was thinking about what he should

say. Finally, he spoke up, "Cum August, ye'll be a man an' ye kin do as ye please, an I won't have no say-so over ye, nohow." He paused, which gave Aint Jidy a chance to start sniffling and wipe her eyes on her apron.

"Try t' tough hit out hyar til we git th' crops laid by, and then ye kin

head West iffen thet's whut ye want t' do."

"I wish to th' Lord Above I'd never sent the girls to beg fer thim papers," Ma said as she brushed aside the tears which had started down her face. Aint Jidy sat still as a statue with her mouth shut so tight it looked like her nose was hooked under her chin. It seemed to me she had gone from looking like a little white hen to resembling a big old hoot-owl.

"Now, Phoebe," Pa said getting up from his chair to pat Ma's shoulder, " ye know ye cain't keep th' young'uns under yore dress tail fer ever."

"No, an' I ain't gone yet," Peter said in a voice designed to ease Ma and Aint Jidy's concerns. He followed Pa to the kitchen door and said, "Let's go finish up th' work over in th' pasture."

Sometime during the afternoon Aint Jidy pasted a new page over the advertisement and nothing more was said about the matter. But the seed had been sewn and one day in late September Peter announced he was setting out on his great adventure to the Golden West.

All of us young' uns cried to see him go, although we were excited that we'd get to see him off on the train and spend a pleasant day in Echo City. Not long after Peter's tear-filled departure, there was a day of rejoicing when we got his first letter postmarked San Francisco, California. Aint Jidy took the envelope in her ands, held it to her lips and kissed it over and over, saying, "Bless the Lord, Peter my child."

Ma opened the letter and read it aloud. Peter wrote that he had gotten a good job with Thomas & Thomas and, while his new life was different from it was like back on the farm, it was "almost as good." He told Pa about the kind of fertilizer he was selling and how it was "different" from what we used on the farm. This, of course, gave Pa a good, hearty laugh but it made Aint Jidy "tch, tch" to show her disapproval.

We missed Peter most at night during the dreary winter months when we gathered around the tin heater.. Us young'uns recalled how Peter's endless supply of wise-cracks -- "they may whip our cream but they'll never beat our milk," or one of his favorite sayings,, " you don't have to hang from a tree to be a nut," and "

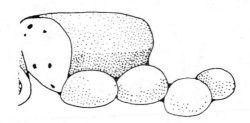

you may be white-bread in Tennessee, but y'er jest a crumb

aroun' here."

Peter also entertained us with rhymes he either made up or

heard from his friends. One day when Pa brought home a

round of cheese, Peter told us, "Cheese, you know, is a

peevish elf. It digests everything but itself!"

And all of us girls, of course, loved to jump rope to chants

we learned mostly from Peter.   Lily May and I never tired

of skipping rope while reciting,

"Cinderella, dressed in yellow

"Went downstairs to kiss a fellow

"By mistake, she kissed a snake
"How many doctors did it take...
"1, 2, 3, 4..."

Shortly before he left for the Golden West, Peter taught us

a new rhyme and it quickly became our favorite:

"Granny, will your dog bite?
No, child, no.
Your Daddy cut his biter off a long time ago,
Granny, does his tail wag?
No, child, no,
Your daddy cut his wagger off a long
time ago,
Granny, how could you let him do
such things?
'Cause, child, your Daddy is the ruler
of all kings."

Although he was gone, Peter left behind enough riddles,

songs and foolish sayings to keep us laughing through the

cold, snowy winter. And while we envied him his new life

in the city, the truth was none of us would have traded our

snowy "holler in th' mountains" for Peter's "Golden West".

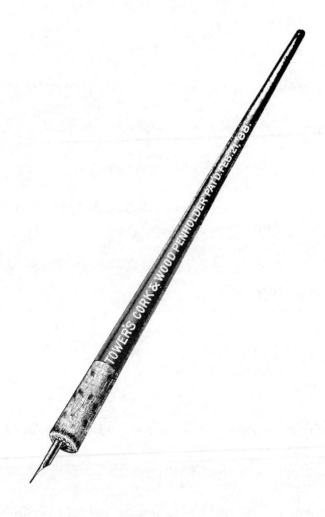

Back From The Golden West

Peter had been away for so long it seemed at times like he'd never been with us at all. In truth, he had been in California for just over two years, but to me if felt like forever. Of course, he wrote often and almost always enclosed a five dollar bill which made our life easier. Whenever a letter appeared from Ma's "little boy in the Golden West", there was always a sense of excitement and we always looked for news from Peter.

In a recent letter he told us he was doing well, and, in fact, had "almost struck it rich." He enclosed a ten dollar bill in place of the usual five` and in his next lettter there was a crisp, new $20 dollar bill. This was the most money I'd ever seen, but even more exciting than the shiny, new bill was what Peter had written: "Ma, you and Pa and Aint Jidy and everyone else will be happy to know I have taken unto myself a little woman. Her name is

Constantinople Regina Manolides and she works at the firm as a bookeeper."

Ma and Aint Jidy whooped after Ma read this part out loud, and Aint Jidy huffed, "with a big name like thet I be a Buffalo Quarter she'll be snooty an' so citified ain't no one will be able to stand

her"Like as not," Ma conceded, "an' we know citified folk don't much like country life one bit. Why, she might likely say we're hillbillied."

"Phoebe," said, frowning at Ma and Aint Jidy, " ye an' Jid will have Peter's woman shot an' her bones scattered over these hyar hills a' fore ye ever set yer eyes on her. Why don'cha wait 'til Peter brings her t' see us an' then ye kin see whut she thinks about us. Jest 'cause she has a long name... why look at Vangie here, her name is might' near as long."

"Yeh, yer right, Pa", Ma conceded right away, :Peter might never come back iffen she's got sech a big job thar, so we'll wait an' see an' iffen she cums fer a visit, then we kin size her up proper." "Well, I have never been one to run a person down a'fore I have a chance t' size her up nohow,"Aint Jidy said smugly. "I jest hope an' pray Peter comes t' see us before I pass int' th' Great Beyond." As she said "Great Beyond" Aint Jidy folded her hands across her bosom and raised her eyes to the ceiling.

"Well, I'm shure Peter'll cum back a'fore ye pass," Pa said, and then he smiled and added, " 'though none o' us kin know fer sartain they'll take ye in.""Now, Roger, don't be funnin' yer sister," Ma scolded him. "A saintly person like Jid is bound fer Glory an' ye an I both know hit. But before Jidy departs, I'm sure Peter will return, iffen hit be the Lord's will. I know Peter an' I know he'l want t' show his little woman."

Ma's words pleased everyone and we stopped talking about Aint

Jidy "passing" and started talking about his good fortune, his little woman and the liklihood of a visit.

"One thing I want t' say t' ye all," Aint Jidy spoke with firmness, "is let's all try not t' talk hillbilly talk no more. Ye know hit's what city folks calls hit an' iffen Con-stan-tye-no-pearl hears th' way we talk, she's apt to say we're 'backwoods'."

"Jid," Pa objected, "ain't ye takin' note don't none of us talk like we use 't?"
"Yeh, with th' young 'uns in school they hear th' way folks in Echo City talk an' we git so we sound jest like thim," Ma agreed with Pa.

"Well, Roger, all I wuz tryin' t' point out is we'd do well t' take notice of how we talk, a'fore Peter shows up with his little woman who ain't never bin out in th' country."

131

"Well, th' times have changed," Pa admitted, "but even if Peter's little woman don't like th' way hit cums out when I talk, I ain't goin' change one bit. I'm bound t' be myself an' ye kin put thet in yer pipe an' smoke hit!"

"There's times when I wish't thet time hadn't changed," Ma said wistfully. "We used t' have a housefull o' young 'uns an' now Peter's gone off t' the Golden West an done grow'd and marr'ed. An' Sister Cecile's got th' set o' twins an' Huddy Lou. Lily May's run off an' marr'ed Ebie an' her not but fourteen years old, and

Amy, Peggy-Jean Ruth, Vangie an' the rest will up an' marry a'fore ye kin say, "what's in yer pouch, what's in yer house, give me a twirl an' turn me about!"

Pa laughed and said, "I ain't heard anybody say thet since I wuz a shaver. But ycr right, Phoebe, th' times has changed an' us with them."

A month went by after we got Peter's letter. Then I went to the bright red mail box Pa had just put up by the side of the road and found a second letter from Peter! I took out the letters the postman had left for us, but I didn't dare open it. Ma had given strict instructions we were never to open Peter's letter, since we might lose the money he always sent.

I ran into the kitchen where Ma and Aint Jidy were cooking and talking.

"Ma. Ma. Ye got a letter from Peter!" I shouted as I handed her the envelope with the San Francisco address on it. Ma ripped open Peter's latest letter, smiled when she found the crisp ten dollar bill inside, and quickly put it in her apron pocket. She began to read and, then with a whoop, she yelled, "he's comin' home! he's comin' home!"

Now it was Aint Jidy's turn to shout, "Praise th' Lord! Praise th' Lord! My boy is comin' home!" Then the big smile which had lit up her face turned to a scowl, "Phoebe, we won't never be able t' fix up this place in time."

"Yeh, hit's hard t' know whut t' do fust," Ma agreed and then both she and Aint Jidy began to sob.

"Whut on earth's wrong with th' two o' ye?" Pa asked as he charging through the open kitchen door.

"Peter's comin' home," Ma explained between sobs.

"An' there ain't no way we kin git th' house fixed up in time," Aint Jidy added as she wiped her eyes on her apron.

"When's he comin'?" Pa asked.

"He didn't say 'xactly but he said he'd send one o' them telegrams y' let us know."

As Ma, Pa and Aint Jidy were talking, I picked up Peter's letter, to read for myself:

> Dear Mother and Folks,
>
> I am writing to tell you I will be seeing you in a few weeks.
> I'm bringing Constaninople east to see you. I will send you
> A telegram telling you when to expect us.
>
> Your Loving Son,
>
> Peter

I put the letter back in the envelope and Ma grabbed it up to add to

all the other letters from Peter which she kept in a little red box that sat on the fireboard.

Ma said, "we've got t' git crackin' an' git things fixed up. Peter's bringing his woman here so we need t' clean this place 'til hit shines Th' fust thing we gotta do is git some store-bought lye!"

The next two weeks were spent cleaning, fixing up and hiding stuff in the barn. Ma had us scrub both the front and back porches with the lye and kept us at it until the floor boards were white as chalk

Then Ma had us paste up new catalog pages on the kitchen wall. The boys were sent to fetch straw while we carried out the feather beds to air in the sun. Aint Jidy stuffed the ticks till their seams looked full enough to burst,.

"Ma, yer workin' us so hard if Peter don't come soon, we'll all be dead!" Lily-May complained and I silently agreed with her.

We had to admit, though, the house sparkled like never before, and when Pa came in that afternoon he had the bright yellow telegram from Western Union.

Although we knew it was from Peter, getting our very first telegram nearly scared us all to death.

"Hit seems, somehow er other, gittin' a telegram jest make ye think somebody has died," Ma said, wiping biscuit dough from her hands. "Ever' blessed time hits one of thim yeller en-ve-lopes hit sez, "sorry t' advise yoou yore Uncle Lonnie Gee passed away last evening."

"Phoebe, he passed away more'n two years ago," Pa snorted as he handed her the telegram.

"I know, I know," Ma said, "I wuz jest sayin' when Western Union shows up, most often someone has died. I kin see this is from Peter, but I'm still a'fear'd t' open hit."

"Well, I ain't a'feard," I said as I took the envelope from Ma's hands and tore it open. But when I pulled out the yellow sheet, Ma took it back and said, "iffen this sez somebody er other has died, I reckon I wan t' be th' fust t' know hit."

"Well, read hit so all kin know," Aint Jidy urged.
"San Franciso, California. July 7, 1921. Time: 2:30 a.m. Will arrive Echo City by train Saturday July 16 at 4 p.m. Stop. Love, Peter

Although we had known for weeks that Peter was comng home, the telegram made it real. Ma said, "hit's been so long since we've seen our eldest, I reckon I'll turn plum' crazy, like as not."
"No ye won't," Pa said, "folks jest naturally love hit when one of their loved ones comes home. Hit said the sixteenth an' thets jest two days from now."

By now Aint Jidy was so excited she was red in face, breathing hard and her bosom heaving. That evening when I pulled the old

churn dasher up and down, it seemed to say, "Peter is comin', Peter is comin'."

Tom-Willie said the tea-kettle sounded to him like a train and made him think about the train station in Echo City.

When Saturday morning arrived, we could talk about nohing but Peter and his little woman. Pa got ready to go to Echo City to meet the train, " I 'spect I'd best not take th' buggy. Peter might be too citifed to ride in hit."

"Hit'd be a good one on him iffen you wuz t' show up with th' hosses an' buggy when they cum off th' train," Ma said, "but

Constantinople might be a'feared o' hosses an' she might not want t' ride in th' buggy."

"No, don't take th' buggy," Aint Jidy said, "ye might fright her. Git Joe Lane's taxi car t'carry them out in.

At one that afternoon Pa left the house saying he had to buy some horse shoe ails and harness oil and a few other supplies. The he'd see if Joe would swap use of the taxi car for a pound of butter. Ma spent almost the entire day cooking while Aint Jidy went through the house making certain nothing had been overlooked. We were expecting Sister Cecile and Toady, Amy and Rufus, Lily-May and Ebie, plus all the young'uns – Huddy Lou, Remanuel and Bedaniel. Peter hadn't seen his nieces and nephews so everyone was excited.

When he heard Joe's taxi car chugging to a stop at the front gate, we knew they had come. Tom-Willie slipped in behind the stove and said, "I'll jest wait here," but Ma told him to come out on the porch with the rest of us to welcome his oldest brother and new wife.

Pa was first out of the taxi car, followed by Peter and then a very large lady wearing the biggest hat I'd ever seen.

"Is that his 'little' woman, ye reckon?" Ma whispered to Aint Jidy. "She must be, an' iffen hit is, she's his little baby elephant! I declare thet lady is th' equal of Sister Thornberry!" Aint Jidy replied, covering her mouth with her hand.

We walked out to the gate to greet them and Ma went running to Peter, wailing, "Son, son, oh Lord, yer crippled! How'd ye hurt yerself? How long have ye had t' use a cane?"

"Ma, I'm fine," Peter smiled, "this is just the style to carry a 'walking stick.'" He showed her a fancy black cane with a gold top.

"Heaven forbid!" Aint Jidy gasped, "he's turned into a city slicker!"

It turned out that for once Aint Jidy was correct. We couldn't get over the way Peter talked when he said he wanted to "take note that all of the youngsters were so well turned out."

Ma and Aint Jidy agreed that "Constance" – Constaninople was "pretty as a picture," but I was the only one who overheard Aint Jidy mutter under her breath, "as a matter of fact, she cud make TWO pictures!"

Ma led them into the "guest room." This is what we'd heard city folks called a "company room." Ma said she wanted to be as up-to-date and modern as anyone who lived in the big city, and Peter's "little woman" wouldn't have a thing on us.

"We keep this room fer th' guest room," Ma explained to

Constaninople, "an we allus like hit best fer th' guests so they kin see clear t' th' road from th'front winder."

Constaninople said it was a very pretty room indeed, and she would certainly "admire the rural view." Then she made a big fuss over the pink, white and yellow crepe paper roses sitting on the center table, and this, of course, pleased Aint Jidy no end since she had made them.

I could tell from the way Ma fluttered about she was very nervous. She smoothed the bed covers and confided, "there's a brand new straw tick on here, an' we sunned th' feathers good, too. I bet'cha ye ain't never laid on straw an' feathers a'fore, did ye?"

Constaninople smiled and said no she'd never had the pleasure but it surely looked "inviting."

"Well, I'm goin' on sixty," Aint Jidy declared, "an' I ain't never

laid on eny other kind, an' I don't mind tellin' ye, I ain't aimin' t' neither." She set her mouth in a firm line as she finished speaking.

We helped put Constaninople's things in the guest room dresser, and then we joined the men on the front porch. Peter was saying,

"You know, the old homestead looks so different to me." As we all found a seat, Constantinople went over to Peter and whispered in his ear.

"Father," Peter announced, "Connie would like to have a ride on a horse. She's never ridden before."

"Well, we'll jest have t' give her a twirl," Pa said, but I could tell he was trying to decide which one of our old horses could carry

that much weight. So Pa, Peter and "Connie" went out to the barn and pretty soon I could hear shouts and much laughter. Aint Jidy started to say something about city slickers but stopped and went off to the kitchen instead without saying another word.

Supper that evening was every bit as exciting as when Ma fixed our victuals for the Big June Meeting. Ma had boiled a ham and fried up two big fryers with a pan of gravy. Aint Jidy had made her special recipe of cornmeal yeast-bread and outdone herself with a five layer white cake with caramel icing.

When supper was almost ready, we heard Toady's car.

When they came in everyone began hugging and kissing and Ma and Aint Jidy began to cry.

"I do declare," Aint Jidy said, "iffen I do say so myself, them are th' prettiest young 'uns o' Sister Cecile's I laid my two eyes on!"

Woodrow Wilson came running in yelling, "Lily-May an' Ebie are comin' up th' road on Ebie's blind mule."

"How does a blind mule know which way to go? Connie asked.

Peter laughed and Ma explained that Ebie's mule made up for

being blind by having "horse sense." Aint Jidy nodded and told Amy and me the mule likely had more of that than Ebie did.

Everyone continued to talk at once and laugh and cry throughout the dinner. Peter had been gone for so long it seemed there were no end of stories to tell. Pa recalled how he'd been in town the day Brother Who died, and Connie's eyes grew big and round when Pa described how they found him under the train. We told them about Aint Jidy's prize at the Fair and the Preacher's fine sermon when Isaac "passed" and both Peter and Pa had extra helpings of the ham and chicken as we talked.

 At midnight Ma said she and Pa hadn't been up so late since Isaac Perry died. Pa was already nodding in his chair and Aint Jidy had been sound asleep with her mouth open for half an hour. Ma told us although she hated to see the day end, it was time for bed. As she started up the stairs she turned, "this is the one day I will remember so long as I am on this Earth." Then, completely forgetting to talk like a city person, she went on, "Vangie, put this hyar slopjar in th' front bedroom fer Peter an' Con-stan-TI-no-pul," she sounded just like her old self.

Everyone smiled as she roused Pa and he woke Aint Jidy, telling her, "Time t-git t'bed."

Pa yawned, stratched his head and then his backside, as he said, "Ye know when a feller has all o' his young 'uns 'round him, an' he's jest polished off a good meal an' had a good nap, I'd say he's as well of as eny King. Th' good Lord has seen fit t' smile down on us, an' I ain't 'shamed t' tell ever' one o' ye how happy ye've made yer ol' Pa on this day."

Ma nodded her head in agreement and said, "Pa ye'll allus be king o' this roost but iffen we don't git these young 'uns t'bed, won't none of us be worth tarnation tomorrow." Pa smiled at Peter, Aint Jidy, Constaninople and all the rest of us as he followed Ma up the

stairs to bed. He stopped at the top step and looked down at all of us, "Th' Pine clan is blessed thet th' Good Lord brung us all back t'gether on this day an' hit's a true blessin' we all kin lay our contented souls down an' sleep happy."

Need A Gift?

For

- Shower • Birthday • Mother's Day •
  • Anniversary • Christmas •

Turn Page for Order Form
(Order Now While Supply Lasts!)

To Order Copies

. We Pay Shipping .

Please send me _____ copies:
$9.95 each. (Make checks payable
to **QUIXOTE PRESS**.)

Name _____

Street _____

City _____ State _____ Zip _____

Hearts 'N Tummies Cookbook Co.
1854 - 345th Ave.
Wever, IA 52658
800-571-2665

- -

To Order Copies:

. We Pay Shipping .

Please send me _____ copies
$9.95 each. (Make checks payable
to **QUIXOTE PRESS**.)

Name _____

Street _____

City _____ State _____ Zip _____

Hearts 'N Tummies Cookbook Co.
1854 - 345th Ave.
Wever, IA 52658
800-571-2665